THE STILLNESS, THE DANCING

Also by Linda Bierds

Flights of the Harvest-Mare (1985)

THE STILLNESS, THE DANCING

POEMS BY
Linda Bierds

An Owl Book

HENRY HOLT AND COMPANY   NEW YORK

Published by Henry Holt and Company, Inc.,
115 West 18th Street, New York, New York 10011.
Published in Canada by Fitzhenry & Whiteside Limited,
195 Allstate Parkway, Markham, Ontario L3R 4T8.

Library of Congress Cataloging-in-Publication Data
Bierds, Linda.
The stillness, the dancing : poems / by Linda Bierds.
—1st ed.   p.   cm.
"An Owl book."
ISBN 0-8050-0766-0 (pbk.)
I.   Title.
PS3552.I357S7   1988
811'.54—dc19   88-9603
                                                       CIP

Grateful acknowledgment is made to the editors of the following
magazines and anthologies, where poems first appeared:

The Bloomsbury Review: "Within the Horse Latitudes"; *Crossing
the River: Poets of the American West:* "Child in the Wagon,"
"Pt. Barrow"; *Field:* "The Neon Artist in December," "Won-
ders," "Quickly and Fully"; *New England Review:* "From the
Ghost, the Animal," "Off the Aleutian Chain"; *The New Yorker:*
"Pearl," "Reviving the Geyser: Reykjavík, Iceland, 1935," "The
Klipsan Stallions," "Strike," "The Anatomy Lesson of Dr. Nico-
laas Tulp: Amsterdam, 1632," "Erebus," "Wedding"; *Poetry
Northwest:* "Winter Fire: Minneapolis," "The White Ponies";
Seattle Arts: "Pt. Barrow"; *Seattle Review:* "The Claude Glass:
1890," "The Genius, Inaudi."

Some of the poems in this volume appeared in a chapbook, *Off
the Aleutian Chain,* L'Épervier Press, 1985.

First Edition

Designed by Susan Hood
Printed in the United States of America
10 9 8 7 6 5 4 3 2 1

In memory of my father

HENRY WALTER BIERDS

Contents

A horizontal line is used to indicate a space between stanzas of a poem wherever such spaces are lost in pagination.

PART 1

THE STILLNESS, THE DANCING

I am indefinitely capable of wonder.
                              —Federico Fellini

Long ago, in the forests of southern Europe,
just south of Mâcon, a woman died in childbirth.
She was taken, by custom, to the small slate
lip of a mountain. Legs bound at the knees
she was left facing west, thick with her still child.

Century by century, nothing disturbed them

so that now
the bones of the woman cup the small bones
of the child: the globe of its head angled
there, in the paddle and stem of her hips.

It is winter, just after midday. Slowly,
shudder by civilized shudder, a train slips over
the mountain, reveals to its weary riders

something white, then again, something
white at the side of the eye. They straighten,
place their lips to the glass, and there, far
below, this delicate, bleached pattern,
like the spokes of a bamboo cage.

What, someone whispers, and What, What,
word after word bouncing back from its blossom
of vapor, the woman and child appearing,
disappearing, as the train slips down through the alders—
——

until they are brands on the eyelid, until they are
stories, until, thick-soled and silent,
each rider squats with a blessing of ocher.

And so there are stories. Mortar. A little stratum
under the toenails. A train descends from a mountain,
levels out, circles a field where a team of actors
mimics a picnic. The billowing children.
On the table, fruit, a great calabash of chilled fish.
And over it all, a beloved uncle, long mad,
sits in the crotch of an oak tree.

He hears to his right, the compressed blare
of a whistle—each sound wave approaching shorter, shorter,
like words on a window, then just as the engine passes,
the long playing out.
He smiles as the blare seeps over
the actors, the pasture, the village

where now, in the haze of a sudden snowfall,
a film crew, dressed for a picnic, coaxes a peacock
to the chilled street. Six men on their knees
chirruping, laughing, snow lifting in puffs
from the spotlights. And the peacock,
shanks and yellow spurs high-stepping, high-stepping,
slowly unfolds its breathless fan, displays
to a clamor of boxcars, clubcars—

where riders, excited,
traveling for miles with an eyeful of bones
see now their reversal.

In an ecstasy of color the peacock dips,
revolves to the slow train:
each rider pressed to a window,
each round face courted in turn.

THE KLIPSAN STALLIONS

Just one crack against the sandbar
and the grain freighter crumbled into
itself like paper in flames, all the lifeboats
and blankets, the tons of yeasty wheat
sucked down so fast the tumbling sailors

still carried in the flat backs of their brains
the sensations of the galley, smoky with mutton fat,
someone's hiccup, someone's red woolen sleeve
still dragging itself across their eyes

even as the long sleeve of the water closed over them.

It was 3 A.M., the third of November, 1891.
Just to the south of this chaos, where the Columbia
washes over the Pacific,

there was shouting, the groan of stable doors,
and over the beachfront, a dozen
horses were running. Trained
with a bucket of timothy to swim rescue,
they passed under the beam of the Klipsan lighthouse,
passed out from the grasses, alfalfa,
deep snores and the shuffle of hooves,

and entered the black ocean.
Just heads then, stretched nostrils and necks
swimming out to the sailors
who were themselves just heads, each brain

a sputtering flame above the water.
Delirious, bodies numb, they answered
the stallions with panic—
So this is the death parade, Neptune's
horses lashed up from Akasha!—

                                    And still,

through some last act of the self, when
the tails floated past they grabbed on,

then watched as the horses
returned to themselves, as the haunches
pulled, left then right, and the small circles
of underhooves stroked up in unison. Here
was the sound of sharp breathing, troubled
with sea spray, like bellows left out in the rain,
and here the texture of sand on the belly,
on the shirt and thigh, on the foot
with its boot, and the naked foot—and then, finally,
the voices, the dozens gathered to
cheer the rescue, the long bones of the will,
causing hands to close over those rippling tails,
yellow teeth to close over the timothy.

EREBUS

Even in the rigging there is chaos,
the foremast and mainmast square-rigged,
the mizzenmast and jibs fore-and-aft rigged, so their lines
cut in at slants, sharp and terrifying,

like the slant-lights of the Scriptures.

And their flurry is extended to the deck,
where snow curls up with the chocks.
By midnight the waterbuckets freeze, each claiming
at dawn a wafer of thumbskin, peeled back

from its slick under-mate like the eyelids of the dying.
We are just below forty now: Franklin, Fitzjames,
the surgeons, ice-master, thirty seamen, and cook.
And a small bird the color of celadon,
of the hummocks and fog-green fjords stumbling
off from the shoreline. It carries just under a wing
a circle of fuchsia down, blinking out
now and then like our lost sun.

Northwest Passage! Not even a harbor. Barrow Strait,
Boothia, Cape Felix. And the days are lessening.
We inch to the south as the icebergs themselves inch off
from the main-pack: the crack and rustle,
the slow letting go.

What world is this that tightens under us—
each time the wind recedes, freezes

under us, leaving just our small bouquet
of masts and grindstones, a hogshead of sugar?

Now and then, ice-locked in this awkward
and constant half-light, we walk over the floes,
watch the simple flight-strokes of snow bunting,

then carry their image to our own companion.
It washes its wings in cabin air.
As the fuchsia circle blinks out, again and again,
we practice our game of resemblances, creeping
closer to all we have been:

God's eye, someone offers. Or ember.
Raw thumb! A taffeta underskirt.
Or the blossom a bullet might leave,
on its journey to a darker harbor.

WITHIN THE HORSE LATITUDES

We were not the first. The entire corridor
was named for this.

—Captain Mathew Baird,
   Navigating the Horse Latitudes: 1750

Again, no wind.
The day burns and burns.
Again the shadows of slack sails
droop over the Atlantic.

Compressed at the center of this stillness,
arid and load-heavy, the ship
cups its panic like an oval flame.
Someone is weeping. On his gums
are the spongy blisters of scurvy,
and around him, on deck,

twenty horses scraping haunches, twirling
stunned white eyes back over their shoulders.
There is shouting, the command of gunfire,
black hooves clacking past a gap in the railing,
then stroking, mid-air, even before
the bodies submerge,

surface to become their own pure symbols:
chaos and instinct.
It is this the sailors turn from—
white water, the terrible bleat, twenty
necks thumping the sideboards—not death, but

the intrusions of absolute chaos, instinct.
In a slow line

they return to the hold, where the odor of
horses has not diminished.
There is darkness, almost a twilight.
Alfalfa pale in its still pattern.
The sailors stop, close their eyes for an instant,

and this emptiness might be a paddock,
horses just beyond, nudging the fence beams,
the beautiful cycles of replenishment
about to begin. Deep in this half-lit
and perfect silence, they stop, close their eyes,
and here is the land of their birth after all,
its water simple and everywhere.

WINTER FIRE: MINNEAPOLIS

The way a table—white pine or fir, a husk
of clear lacquer—darkens
each day in a sunny kitchen,
melanin and light interacting until
the ghost-shapes of placemats appear,

so the white vinyl floor
tans yellow, then amber, in the seconds
before it blackens, before the rubber faces
of dolls collapse, wash away
in this alien licking.

So cold the hoses cough frost.
Then clear. All across new snow
the wind-blown ashes hook in. And
where the house is not burning—flung up
past the porch and handrail—
a tassel-cape of ice.

Some collision of mythic symbols,
of course, this fire, this ice.
And yet on the sidewalk, a woman holds
her daughter's arm, sees the pale terry pattern
of bathrobe, and above, breath
with its grief-pulse.

Their kitchen is burning, soon
the bedrooms and small parlor. In a flurry
of the intricate, corn kernels burst

from their casings, milk
and the ruby molecules of vinegar burst.

Burning. All the details of their lives,
all the *pieces:* napkins and window frames, tiny
spiderings of plaster under picture hooks.
And the molding: white rods
of pine, hand-clipped,
hand-stained one night on a nest of newsprint,
stroke after soft stroke, each
beautiful pore darkening.

THE WHITE PONIES

Commander R. F. Scott
b. June 1868
d. South Pole Exploration Party, March 1912

No color at all now
and wind kicking up the snow to a blizzard.
Four men, six sleds, ponies
so white they are nothing.

A mistake, the leader thinks, how
the hooves slip and the clear, frightening bay
scoots over the ice forever.

He watches the reins shimmy,
remembers his father far ahead on the bank
of the Thames, an incredible tow rope
looped over his shoulders like a harness.
Pulled by that rope, how the skiff
veered to the shoreline, while the boy inside
pushed off with a birch stick,
watched his father jog on, appearing,
disappearing as the river turned.

And so, through memory, this landscape
takes its texture, its color. There is coughing,
the faint lisp of the runnerblades.
We have stood at the axis of the world,
someone shouts, all boots pointing north
and a tug on the trousers like the undertow
of the Black Sea!
                    He laughs, looks

over his shoulder at the others.
And why do you climb the mountain,
he teases, and why do you cross the road?

Snow lessens
then sky returns with its white covering.
Near death, a pony stumbles.
And because there is no night here,
for weeks now, months, the men just unroll
their brittle pallets, rest in the open daylight.

A little wind ruffles the weather bags.
All the compasses in our hands just slackened,
someone thinks, as if we were the source they were seeking.

And how beautiful the ponies are:
white outlines of the bodies, appearing, disappearing
on a backdrop of snow. For warmth,
they graze over the resting men,
who awaken now and then to the long faces,
eyes fixed and liquid like rheumy moons.
Such wonder, someone calls, such curiosity we contain
to be pulled by the likes of you!

There is laughter. Behind clouds,
the sun moves in its high arc over this region—
without birds, without lichen or moss, without night—
over this landscape, this acceptance of nothing but
light. From his pallet, the leader waits, watches
the sky, the occasional interruption of an animal face,
breath lifting up from the nostrils.
Father, he thinks, when the shoreline turned
you were nothing—just steam, the rope
held taut by steam.

PT. BARROW

She was lactating. We know this
by the right, swollen breast.
By the swollen bladder, the lank stomach,
we know it was early morning.

So the hours become these hours.

An arctic storm, rare in the springtime,
scales sod from a dome
fattened
by the amber, marrow-filled bones of the gray whale.
Beneath it, a woman,
a man and small child are sleeping.

It is 1600.

The woman wakes to a yawl of cracking whalebones.
At the beach below her shelter, the onshore wind,
the flood-tide, the sea-ice melting for weeks

combine in a statement of preservation.

Nothing in her world has sounded like this, has
pressed like this. She is lifted,
tasting salt. Slowly, her stiffened walrus blanket
leaves ridges on her buttocks.

We trace them.

———

We trace the ragged blossoms of seal-smoke
blackening her lungs.

There is sperm stalled at the lip of her cervix.
And here,

on her shoulder,
a dozen shallow trenches, scratched
by the ornamental claws of a walrus blanket, that

chafed, chafed,
that just before midnight, rolled off

with her spent husband, like
a black bear, comic, mottled with light.

Surely she spoke then. Surely

the child, keeping sleep, took
her language to a dream, gave it
motion, shape,
hurled its icy, perfect body into the hours.

PART 2

FROM THE GHOST, THE ANIMAL

Of all the figures in delirium tremens,
the most common is the gray dog.

Not the rat then. We assumed it was the rat,
scratching up not hell exactly, but
the path there. We assumed
it was the spider, leech,
each in from its Gothic other, those zones
with us and not, like sleep.

But the dog, gray dog—
flock-guider, companion for the slow
rowing—pads in from the hallway,
your life in tow.
                    And please,
there is something wrong with the light,
this muzzle, honed to a trowel,
this jab, retreat, this
dirge through a smile of froth. Up
from your ribs, lungs, up
from the hollows you walk through—

wind, black shoe, the sun at your eyelids,
the simple bread—up from the ghost
and the animal, you answer—bellow,

hideous whine—while he slumps to the floorboards,
clear-eyed, pants *Run*
with me darling, the meadows, the lost day.

CHILD IN THE WAGON

The child in the wagon remembers a sound:
leaves that clicked down the cobblestones
like the toenails of running dogs.
It was evening. She turned, expecting the worst,
and found instead the swirl of madrona leaves
and then on the street corner
candle flames cupped in their glass boxes.

I will not hear that sound again, she thinks,
and looks to her left, right,
where the long Conestoga wagons bumble
through the switchgrass. There are forty, indigo
and red, moving not single file but *abreast,*
their hoops and canvas hoods swaying white, and
seen from above, the child thinks, like a wave
spilling into the harbor, its line of froth
and the dust swelled up behind like a second wave.

So the pattern continues, until day ends
and the center wagons stall, all their horses
simply stepping in place as the end wagons
arc toward one another and the wagoners
on their lazyboards draw up
their perfect circle, like the nets of Maine fishermen.
That evening, near sleep on the floorboards,
the child describes to her parents
the sound of madrona leaves, running dogs.
How, for an instant, fear passed through her
like an icy tooth—the long-haired sea dogs

rushing in from the ships—
and then there was nothing: leaves, a certain peace.

And that sound . . . like this? her mother whispers,
clicking knives to a pewter cup. Then the father—
who will die in October, his cheeks in miniature
the caved salt cliffs they are leaving—
begins, tapping this, that, this, that,
until the wagon, in its circle of wagons, fills.
And there on the canvas, the child thinks,
how beautiful the hand shadows are:
great moths come in from the wilderness.
Like this? they ask. Like this?
As if in a moment, the absolute sound
might appear—then the dogs rush past, thick with loss.
And there would be peace.

WONDERS

In a wide hoop of lamplight, two children—
a girl and her younger brother—jump marbles
on a star-shaped playboard. Beside them,
in a chair near a window, their father
thinks of his mother, her recent death

and the grief he is trying to gather.
It is late October. The hooplight spreads
from the family, through the window,
to the edge of a small orchard, where
a sudden frost has stripped the fruit leaves
and only apples hang, heavy and still
on the branches.

The man looks from the window, down
to a scrapbook of facts he is reading.
The spider is proven to have memory, he says,
and his son, once again, cocks his small face
to the side, speaks a guttural oh, as if
this is some riddle he is slowly approaching,
as if this long hour, troubled with phrases
and the queer turn in his father's voice,
is offered as a riddle.

There is the sound of marbles
in their suck-hole journeys, and the skittery
jump of the girl's shoe
as she waits, embarrassed, for her father
to stop, to return to his known self, thick

and consistent as a family bread.
But still he continues,

plucking scraps from his old book, old
diary of wonders: the vanishing borders
of mourning paper, the ghostly shape
in the candled egg, beak and eye
etched clearly, a pin-scratch of claw.

A little sleet scrapes at the window.
The man blinks, sees his hand on the page
as a boy's hand, sees his children bent over
the playboard, with the careful pattern
of their lives dropping softly away, like
leaves in a sudden frost—how the marbles
have stalled, heavy and still on their fingers,
and after each phrase the guttural
oh, and the left shoe jumping.

STRADIVARI

Like infants:
bellies and backs, the curling
waist-ribs. Unglossed, laid body to body
on the ponderous table, their juiced and thready fibers
dry, pull up. . . .

The workroom is chilled with morning.
A little ground fog outside
repeats itself in the scurries of dormice.
And in these waist-ribs and maple shoulders?
Here is your lost son again—scorched throat,
pale ear with its mussel-shell of blood.

All week he has surfaced beside you,
though you shake your head, and a varnish

of crushed linseed calls back the day.
How softly the gouge strokes over the excesses,
tiny quarter-curls of phloem and age-line.
One slip, and the notes
will drop short of the barbers' row,
will rest like a grating of pine dust
on the lips of the surgeons.

The pin-scratch of masts reaching up from the Po
is echoed in the purfling, its
reach to the lighter edges. Now his form once again.
Eighth inch by eighth inch

the pieces slide, arc together, another day
withdraws from the window, and
surely his image will leave you soon,

the wood returning to simple wood,
its sound, just sound.

ULTIMA THULE

A little candlewax on the thumbnail, liquid
at first, slipping, then stalled to an ice-hood.
Another layer, another, and the child lies back,
his thumb a hummock, his small knuckle
buckled with cracks.

No snow yet, but
the last white meadows of switchwort and saxifrage
mimic it. Already the bears brush back
through the dwarf willows—Hubbart Point, Cape Henrietta
  Maria,
the bay's deep arc flattening, lessening
as land extends through the fast-ice and the seam
of open leads stretches, withdraws.

They have come for the pack floes, for the slow
rafting. And repeat on their white faces, the boy thinks,
the low strokes of the borealis: violet mouths,
madder blue at the eyelids. Perhaps he will walk
to the shoreline—no shore, of course, just miles
of land-fast ice stretched over water, stretched out
to water, the line where each begins

a filament, a vapor. By then the bears will be
sailors, or, far to the north, stalled in their waxy sleep.
He yawns, looks down at his slipper, his floormat
of braided fleece. By then the lights
will be thicker, greens and magentas flashing, rolling in

at times like fog. *To go where nothing lives.*
He turns, settles. To extend a little breath

out over that ice—the white, cumbersome bodies
migrating in reverse with the others, dragging
between them a lifeline, plump and intricate,

like a net, like purse seiners dragging a cork net,
its great arc spiraling, tighter, tighter,
now green in those lights, now blue, now
pink as the boy's ear,
where all night a line of cold
traces the rim, the lobe,
circles down, chills, and recedes.

BENEDICTINE

There was a garden, if I recall, with roses perhaps,
a smear of jasmine. And although I
sat there daily, twice in a short rain,
I cannot remember it now. Just an odor
swaying up the exterior wall,
a certain churning with the seasons.
What I do remember is the night-cot,
staved pine, with a little skin of burlap.
And the slow striving to leave the body, to walk
without swaying, to sleep without turning—
the backbone pressed by a gap in pine boards
as fingers might press a garden bean.
Just a whittling away, a daily paring away
of the human contentments, until
under the temples, over the ears,
a heat pressed like a snug hatband
and the self was lifted! It was then
I would sit in the garden, all the roots
with little hooks, and, as if through a thick glass,
the furious scarlet faces of the flowers.

I left when the change came, the papal slackening
that set us off like stones from a sling.
I relearned the world: lovers, infants,
the scrape of the razor on the long thigh.
In a small wood just south of my house
I discovered a silt creek. Often in summer
I wade there, the silt on each foot
like an ocher shoe, and the freeze flaring up

just under the kneecap. And often I think
of the old life: cloister, cell, lost hatband,
the cot with its bony palm. Thick and silent,
each memory carries me easily—although
the garden has released me completely.

A COLLECTOR'S LETTER ON THE LAST

First there were rugs, maroons and blues
from the Caucasus, a notch for prayer,
running dogs at the borders like

beckoning fingers.
Now and then a pattern would break:
some child taking over, some goat
prancing by, knocking an elbow.
I would read, read down the fabric,
then ZIG—and a child was with me.
I stopped. She was gone.
Black hairs and a rubble of sand.
Imagine her dependency

after two hundred years! Zig and
zig. . . . If you were with me

I would take you downstairs, down
a corridor of planks and creosote handrails,
where the truly dependent bask
flat open in a shallow light.
Up from their peat and root-locked boxes
floats the scent of the New World. . . .

To nurture the last of its kind:
a certain buff or rouge, leaves striped
black, white like the flanks of okapis:
to cup it—*the very last*—to offer the graft,
to withhold the graft—there are no responsibilities

———

like these. The genus,
pared down to a filament, just follows the light,
its bead of magenta blossom
opening, closing,
as if the canopy of the world floated overhead.

My colleagues insist that it does!

We sit together like a council of Mesmers,
with infinite distrust and praise.
We understand the paradox of the valuable
in our civilization. How that which
decreases, increases.

You write that to some we are abominable.

This morning I made a shower, perhaps a storm—
no different from the thousand domestic manipulations
of my neighbors. Then I rested.
Just after supper I took
the ceremony of imagination to a dropped leaf:
how the white crumbles first, the black
left lightly behind, stripe after stripe.

Abominable! I am the keeper of
endings and beginnings. I am a small man
with eyeglasses. A lover of plums, the crystalline
countertenor of Deller.

Listen. I will leave you a map when I die.
Take its perfect X's through the forest.
A child will be there when the pattern breaks.
Black hair. Behind her the city, its simple bells.

ADELARD THE DROWNED

from the painting by Marsden Hartley

Your straight-up hair, the little rose behind your ear,
a black bear's chest and hands,
and the hug you gave the pale-eyed, perfumed man,
a black bear's hug. It was Hartley, in from Bermuda,
from the frayed expatriate's spiral—Hamburg,
Veracruz, Dresden, Berlin, Cuernavaca—
the years slipping past with the motion of waves,

spilling out at last to you, your
family of fishermen. A little cinquefoil, then.
Black lobster, and the thick Nova Scotia wind
ruffling your island. How distant his world seemed—
Paris, of course, Taos, but more: that place where form,
where statements on light from the tip of a brush
mattered. And the people, he told you, magical, mutable,
their sibilant names—Stieglitz, Stein, Kandinsky—
milky and lank, like warm-water fish.

To live without wages! Now he could not stop eating,
could not stop cuffing the shallow world,
its brief flirtations. That winter, in furnaces west
of a New York warehouse, he'd watched his paintings
darken, no money for rent, the auctioneer's block
a gavel away. Just smoke, he whispered,
and still, the greens of burning linseed,
the slippery purples of madder-flames

bloomed out again in the brushstrokes of sea flowers.
Such air! You held his waist, taught him

the arc of an oar: knife-thin at first, then a spoon
for the choppy sea. His teeth fell out. One after one.
Until he smiled through the cage of his hand,
head dipped and angled, as if ashamed, as if
the mouth's lost symmetry were an error he made,
a line badly rendered. The long days

drifted. He painted, repainted, blacks, near-blues
built up to pilings, to stones and shore-trees,
massive, weighty in their shapes as . . .
bears! For years to have praised the objective
and now, from the thick strokes of a fir tree,
an arm began, soon your father's face, your chest
and fingers, each simplified shape archaic, mythical.

The moon filled. You stepped closer.
I have not been so near the real thing before, he wrote.
Years yet, until fame came with its wintery blush, but
here was another melding, this mix of your opposite lives.
Humor, intensity. Bravado, reserve. Clay, light.
How far could you carry the fusion?
To the boat? To the storm-plumped waves
you passed through? The sea pushed your pant legs
like so much fluff, your shirt cuffs and cheek flesh rippling,
    thick arms
and legs, weightless, rippling—
overwhelmed in a tangle of water, hair, the ocher-stroked
ear rose closing, opening at once.

THE CLAUDE GLASS: 1890

It is 8:06 in the morning,
a Sunday in August.
Just at this moment, no one is weeping in all of Paris.
The world swirls on its axis, science
blooms, cream is dipped from saucers
with knuckles of ginger-cake.

At the foot of a canopied bed
a man kneels, crosses his wife's cotton stocking
over her garter. He laughs
as the fabric stretches and slides,
the round disk in its metal clip like a sugar tablet.

They have dressed for the country! The basket
is heavy with Brie and oranges,
a Claude glass in a gilt frame.
Such a rage, the man thinks, as they
walk from the wheezing train:
this black mirror in its leafy halo,
its reductions to shadow and light.

And then for an hour he sits, swaying
with the swaying clubcar.
The headrest is lush and sunken,
its sparse velvet pelt surrounding his neck
like the stomach of a spaniel.
There is pipe smoke, the snap
and whisper of cards. Drifting, the man
thinks of a saxhorn from his childhood, then

of lamb chops, his father's face
near death, the hazel, scummed eyes.
Now and then, a river gleams out through the trees.
Soon, when it calms to a green bay,

they will stop—his wife, friends,
the others of their station, brilliant
in cottons and bunting.
All afternoon they will trouble the shoreline,
sometimes wading, sometimes posing in twos, threes
in the flat eye of a Claude glass carried from Paris.

A rage! the man thinks: each family
for an instant historical, each
blowsy collection of heights, a masterpiece—
all around Paris, clumped together
in parks, countryside,
the mirrors tilted this way and that, until
motion and color drop away, until faces
peek out like polished bones, and around them
a Claude Lorrain landscape of hedgerows, black oak trees,
sucks up to a centrum of light.

The man stirs, shakes his head. Near his shoulder
his wife's breathing is deep, rhythmic.
Over her face he watches the window's reflections—
the beeches and steep escarpments,
the foxtails and grasses—flash, flash,
so fast they might be a pulse,
sharp heartbeat of something he cannot name.

DOLL'S HOUSE:
FEDERATION FOREST, 1860

They are broken by the oxen: long cobwebs, strung fir
to sword fern, chickweed to cedar. Far less by the father,
   mother,
just left and behind, or the small daughter, dragging

her feet in the needles. She is thinking
of the water they follow, how a cork dropped there
might move at like speed, and stepping above its bobbing
   path—
in a moment or hour—she *would* cross the same river twice.

They have traveled two years, and each morning
a different canopy! Clouds. Brackbriar. Dry and mite-bitten,
maple leaves puckered like the hands of gnomes.
Now the oxen wait in their own new cloaks,
loose webs, dotted with ground-spores and resin.
Almost beautiful, the child thinks, as the path
she has followed repeats itself in strings

on the swaying dewlaps. Another wagon pulls in. Another.
Far down the line the black germs of diphtheria
speckle lungs and throat-strings. In the still nights
like an echo, how breath from the quarantined wagons—
the scrape and stridor—gives the sound of wagons.

As if she were always arriving. Near sleep, of course,
the night fires shrunken, and yet newly arriving. She lowers

then lifts her head. Hours still, until blankets are opened,
stew pans gleam from the side-hooks. And her father

has fashioned a little door, knee-high, curved at the top,
with a band of eyelet curtain. For the space where the earth
erodes, he told her, where the trunks of firs and cedars
reveal their door-sized caves. And, he had hoped, for fantasy,
that her child's mind might place there in miniature

a family, its calm repetitions. At her back now, a string
of foam as wagons mimic the river. The sunlight is low
on her calves, the tree trunk and wedged door. Behind it,
no hearth or banister, no table or side-chair:
phloem and heartwood, root-flow and a dropping darkness
where light webs in through the curtain, out through the day.

THE WOLVES

We think we can well face death, having
done what we have done.

> —S. A. Andrée, Nils Strindberg,
> *The Complete Record of Their*
> *Balloon Polar Flight, 1897*

The rattling of the guidelines in the snow
and the flopping of the sails
are the only sounds heard, except
for the whining of the basket. . . .

That fills with ice. We cannot stop it,
all the succulent straw taking its ice,
drawing us down, slowly,
slowly, like a bead of honey.

You cannot imagine this whiteness—
sky and earth, our space in between—
and so you imagine:
For me it is the burning of wolves.
Stretched over the glacier, reaching up
from another time, are the fields of Scotland.
There, in threes, fours, women and men
touch torches to a diminishing circle of forest.
Such colors! Quince and magenta,
black wolves leaping out to the slap of muskets.
They have troubled the sheep. At
the moment of impact their bodies snap back,
all the underfur springing up

to the whitest snow!
It is a beauty made perfect by urgency.

It is a beauty *made,* again
and again, as a yellow beaker, lifted
up from its yellow flame,
becomes first a pear, then a jester's tassel.
Beneath it, August Strindberg is weeping.
At his shoulder, the nephew and balloonist, Nils.
The elder writes nothing, but searches instead
for the Transmutation of the Elements,

while the image of the beaker—its pear
and tassel—is delivered to Nils. In our white world
it visits him often, as a tiny sun
or the globe of a torch just muffled
by furze and groundpine. *Uncle, stop,* he writes,

it is we, we are the common denominator.

The trail ropes are lost now,
taking with them our lefts and rights.
We lean on each other. Freezing,
we do not age, yet
the snow ages us daily. Nils,
with the face of Methuselah, the nose hair
and beard iced white . . . and *It is not our act,*
he tells me, *but another's reenactment of it
that gives us immortality!* He laughs.
At the impact of his muscles
his face hair springs back—iced beard,
mustache and eyebrows—
and there, again, he
is the wolf's white belly, both lifting and lifted.

PEARL

First the skip stutters down its rail-line
and the miners, stacked together, knee to knee-back,
stomach to buttock, watch
the clouds, one Douglas fir, a V-tip
of station roof, condense, condense, until
everything they have walked through is a little moon
shining one hundred, one thousand feet,

and exchanged now, from below, for a sparkle
of dusty headlamp—
its growth, like a moon, then
the face and great-boots.

It is always raining. Always
the temperature of sliced ham cooled on a platter,
a placemat, these things of another world.
And unfolded, the miners step into their day, which is
night, walking behind one another
out through the drift tunnels.
An ore cart wobbles by, steaming
with quartz rubble, a little gold perhaps,
the size of a thumbnail, pushed up
from the earth's molten center, through the molten veins,
pushed and pushed—the great pressure, great heat—
to this exact intersection of
vertical, horizontal. . . .

Ears pop.
Someone is singing. And beyond,

from another chamber, comes the whistle of nitrate
billowing up from its spitter fuse.
Now and then some tremble may continue, up
through the ankles, thighs. There is the wheeze
of a bank collapsing, and into the drift tunnel

creep the poisons of powder fumes, methane.
It is then, with the motion of bathers, that
the miners dip into their airmasks, bite
down, and turn together, all
the headlamps reversing their light

to its first horizon.
And nothing can stop what follows,
not science, not the elements:

in a grave interaction of chemicals, saliva,
the airmask biteplates begin heating.
Past the mulch and black-slush, into the skip,
up through the timbers, they grow hotter,
hotter, scorching the tongue,
the palate, until the miners, trapped by a halo
of methane, by the slow pull
of the skip-cable, feel their hearts withdraw, feel
their nerves collect in this new center, foreign
and not—all the flames pushing off,
regathering—the great heat, great pressure—
foreign and not.
But for their eyes, these workers are the color of
quartz rubble, stacked
and lifted ... lifting ... past the shale beds,
limestone, from the rain into the rain ...
and here is that moon, swelling to meet them—
old ghost, old platter of steam—
and here is the world of the world.

PART 3

QUICKLY AND FULLY

homage to Louis Pasteur

Not foam at all. Certainly
not froth. Just a web of viscid gel
palate to muzzle. A squint. A gape. Now and then,
a rush of high-toned howls, sharp, then diminishing.

And where the candlelight offers its own web,
a woman reads of this illness—
one spark of germ, then the brain
like a scarlet skullcap—of the cure she will carry,
those specks of red medulla dictating sound,
flecked, injected, day after day,
two grams of rabid animal brain
flickering through her bloodworks.

Not fury at all. A nudge.
She had carried cold stones down the side-path,
for the licking, the swollen tongue. And out
from a break in the hedgerow, from the nest of
string and balsa, that tongue, nudging a hangnail.

She gathers her gloves,
little kerchief of biscuits and plums.
It is dawn on the roadway to Paris. Already

the chemists are working: all across the room,
suspended from threads in cotton-topped vials,
the daubs of drying medulla wait,
row after row, tiny nerve hooks for hearing, the curl

of the muzzle, used now for madness
turned back on itself—ten-day, five-day, one-day,
to the strongest, far off in a corner,
so plump they might still cup the impulse for sound.

Like glass-harps, she thinks, then takes the injection,
quickly and fully, as she takes the grief,
the little fear, then the joy of human wonder.
Perhaps I will hear as you did—
for these days, the lost animal sounds.
But she does not, of course—just wind
and her shoes in the wheel ruts,
the sluice of bitten plums.

REVIVING THE GEYSER:
REYKJAVÍK, ICELAND, 1935

from a photograph by Jon Dahlman

One man in a derby hat, another
in leggings, and a woman
with the brown, sensible shoes of a chemist.
Just behind these friends
is a thermal circle of
dwarf willow, eyebright, and heath—
and before them, the slack basin,
no hiss and bellow, no steam
hurling up its magnificent stitch.

There is urgency on these faces.
Already the snows creep
closer to this mild setting,
like a ringmaster's animals.

To encourage pressure the man
in the derby hat drops
chunks of pan soap through the quiet water.
They sink like yellow skulls,
and then on the surface

he sees the rippling legs of the woman,
his own small face in its black topknot.
A woodcock sings from a tangle of willow.
The man thinks of his wife at the loom, how
often in the late, thin light her beautiful arms
cross and recross the breast beam

———

with the stroke of a swimmer.
There is pain in his shoulders, in
his pale neck stretched
over the basin. He thinks of a time
when love, in terms of
his place in the world, was everything.

THE STORY

This is the story of a woman,
cerebrally impaired, a bevy of
apraxias, agnosias, who
walked through a theater near London,

through the changing rooms and small alcove,
heels blinking out from her wide shoes
like apricots from a leaf tree,

and stood on the dappled stage. And although
an hour before, her foot could not master
that wide shoe, her key its lock,
her arms their cumbersome sleeves,
still she began:

Why bring back those memories?

It was spring then. Russian soldiers and the wheeze
of a fretsaw. Three sisters—the youngest,
in white, having entered this scene, this
structure, as water might enter a glove. And composed
by the story, its peaks and dips, she became
indistinguishable from the others:
all awkwardness gone, stunted speech
and the clap trap wobble gone,
all the clear multi-spheres of the brain

drawn up in unison
by the story, the pattern of light on a black boot.
Like so many others then, lobe-fractured,

gathered by music, mime,
she was smoothed, perfected: her movements,
tongue, the moods she filled

as she followed the others—
beloved soldiers and sisters—
past the parties, the mummers and pancakes,
listless days, violins, past wealth, boredom, apathy,
to a nibbling grief so wide and unalterable
it might be a tideline.

Gone, she remembered each evening.
Everything's gone. Energy, time, our
place in the world.

How clearly the story held her: another century,
another bevy of losses perfectly retained.
Troikas and ballrooms, grace, inertia,
a certain lamplight, a certain musk-brush of velvet—
from the flurry of latchkeys, woolen sleeves,
the self rushing out, in
to the cupped, transient, dapple-lit
shape of the self.

This is the story of chaos, the ordering
of chaos. Of a woman
held like water in a glove.
Just give me a structure, she said,
its thin, inescapable bones,   ʳ
and I will complete it.

THE GENIUS, INAUDI

The sound the sheep made, lumped together
on the dark hills of Piedmont,
was exactly that of a gate opening
after great time and neglect.
And if it were spring, the man whispers,
say the first of May, say
the year 1020, when that gate
last bleated out its resistance,
it would have been . . . *Wednesday*.

He smiles. This is his favorite time.
Into the ten o'clock night
the audience wanders, happy and stunned,
with just these few remaining.

The air turns rich with cloves and kettle-steam.
Light off the theater seats is the color
of plums. He throws back his huge head,
tells of his childhood as a shepherd, counting
sheep and the visible stars,

tells of the stages in Provence, Amsterdam,
of the pale balsa stages of the White Star liners.
Now and then, he takes from his pocket
a nugget of syrup-filled wax, bites down,
feels the liquid rush out and dissolve,

as the soul, he fears, rushes out and dissolves.
Someone asks for the seconds she has lived,

their roots and powers. All the numbers
are sounds, he explains, without shape.
They come with their perfect order
like a little song.

He closes his eyes, bites down.
In the plum-colored light he is still
and symmetrical: gold buttons side by side
on his velvet jacket, the parallel shoes,
each knee a right angle,

then the hands lifting together
as he tells again of his childhood as a shepherd,
how everything stemmed from that flurry:
the galaxy of sheep, their companion
stars—the world and its complement,
so set and perfect, as he
made his way home through the hills.

THE NEON ARTIST IN DECEMBER

Snow everywhere, like the salt
electrons jump from, as gas snaps
and the tube hisses with light.
I am holding just now the hooked underbeak
of the great flamingo:
cool glass, a little dusting of phosphor.
Just off through the tree-line, the New Year
waits with its bells,

as in the ballroom of the Grand Hotel, stretched
thirty feet up to the promenade deck,
the back-kneed, S-necked mate
waits with its own ringing, its
soft, rattle-whistle of argon.
What a pair they will make: ice-pink tubeworks
north and south on the ballroom floor.
And below: foxscarves, carnations, the pull
and push of the long trombones.

Flamingos! And now
the moon pressing back through the tree-line.

Close your eyes. Let us
say we are children together, ten, perhaps twelve.
I see neon: a steadfast landscape of
DEPOT, HEIDELBERG, VACANCY.
And you? Women in cardigans? A certain
leaf tree? Perhaps the gleam

———

of your dress shoe as you welcome the New Year.
The ballroom is thick with smoke and laughter.
Two birds, of course, north and south. Then
the catch in your breath as an uncle explains
the impact of vapor and salt, how
a light that has never been
curls up through the century—swank,
incredibly still.
Our times, he laughs, and in
from the thin roadways all the WELCOMES,
the PALMISTS and EXITS, all the boneworks
blown to their plush, just bearable tones

curl up to a wing and S-neck.
High above you, cupped
left, right on the ballroom floor, that
ice-pink, still parenthesis.
Then foxscarves. The flick of the black shoes.

WEDDING

from the painting by Jan van Eyck

Wait. The groom stops,
right hand in mid-air, mid-ceremony,
about to descend to the cupped right hand
of the bride. What is that noise?
At their feet, the ice-gray griffin terrier stops.
Two puff-shouldered witnesses just entering
the chamber, just entering the scene
through the iris of a convex mirror,
stop. And follow a curling sight-path
from the elegant to the natural: from the dangling
aspergillum and single ceiling candle, down
past the groom's velvet great-hat, his Bordeaux robe,
past the stiff-tailed lapdog, the empty
crow-toed wooden sandals, to
a trail of yellow apples—desk, ledge, windowsill

and out. *There.* Below. It is
the rasp of water casks on the hunt mares, squeezed
stave pin to stave pin, as
they are shouldered across the canal bridge. And the mares—
how brilliant in the high sunlight:
one roan, one walnut, eight legs
and the rippling ankles rippling again
where the slow Zwin passes under. In a moment

they will cross, step on with their small cargoes
past inns, the great cloth halls steaming with linen.
The mudflats have dried now. All their patterns

of fissures and burls like the rim
of a painter's palette. Once or twice
the cones of yellow flax straw will flicker,
the autumn birch leaves flicker,
the mares lurch left, then

right themselves—nothing to fear after all: not wind, motion.
Not even a sleeve of sackcloth slipped over the hoof.
To quiet the hunt. To make from its little union
not a predator, but a silence.
Just the half-light of forests, black leaves
on their withered stems,
then the graceful, intricate weave closing over
the mossy sole—as a hand might be closed
by a descending hand,
pale, almost weightless, and everywhere.

THE ANATOMY LESSON
OF DR. NICHOLAAS TULP:
AMSTERDAM, 1632

High winter. All canals
clogged with an icy marrow. And the flax—
just a blue wash in the mind of
the painter who puffs up the tower stairs.
It is the time for festival—Aris Kindt
is hanged. And soon

up through these same stairs, up
to the slope-seated deal and chestnut
Theatrum Anatomicum, the surgeons will come:
Mathys and Hartman, Frans, Adriaan,
three Jacobs, then the bleeders and barbers,
the wheelwrights, needle-makers, goldsmiths,
the potters and sculptors, two
thin-chested harehounds. A lesson!
A dissection! All the reverent, mercantile faces
peering off through the scaffolds

that are now just empty,
just a deal and chestnut funnel tapered down
to a corpse:
                Aris Kindt. Quiver-maker.
One necklace of rope-lace curled under his ears—
while over his body, the shadow of a painter's hat
circles, re-circles, like a moth at a candle.

So this is fresh death, its small, individual teeth.

——

Rembrandt walks past the breechcloth, then the forearm
soon to split to a stalk that would be grotesque
but for its radiance: rhubarb tendons
on a backdrop of winter. He swallows,
feels the small dimplings of lunch pork

drop away. And here will be Tulp,
his tweezers and white ruff. And here,
perhaps Hartman, perhaps the shadow of
a violet sleeve closing over the death-face.
It is commissioned: eight faces
forever immortal, and one—slightly waxen—
locked in mortality! He smiles.
How perfect the ears, and the pale eyelids

drawn up from the sockets
like the innerlids of pheasants. Just outside a window,
the day has climbed down to the amber color
of this candlelit room. Rembrandt turns,
crosses out past the sponges and vessels.
There is the sputter of wagon wheels through a fresh ice,
and in all the storefronts
torches hang waiting for a pageant—

scarlet blossoms for a new spring.

His room has turned cold with the slow evening.
Far off in a corner
is a canvas clogged with the glue-skin of rabbits—a wash
of burnt umber, and the whites
built up, layer by layer.
Now a fire, the odor of beets.
And here, where the whites buckle, will be Tulp,
perhaps Mathys, their stunned
contemplation of death. He touches a spoon,

———

then a curve of plump bread. All across his shoulders
and into his hairline winds a little chill,
thin and infinite, like a thread-path
through the stars:
                    there will be umber
and madder root, yellow ocher, bone-black,
the scorch of sulfur, from
the oils of walnut and linseed—all things of the earth—
that forearm, that perfect ear.

RHODOLITE

After so many hours
the shaft gave its own simplicity.
Two colors: earth, the flat amber
candlelight renders.
No more than a dozen sounds:

the thump of the pickaxes,
the suck of the ponies' hooves,
a cough or groan, the clack
and swish of the garnet wagons,

and the echoes of all of these.

Miners arced, then straightened. Ponies
wheezed through their stiffening lungs.
Ax-stroke by ax-stroke, the shaft
crept deeper through dolomite,

light ticking out from the candles,
past posts and headboards,
splayed legs and hand picks, past
the cupped foliations
of limestone, garnet-knots,
to the long blindness of earth.

When the quit-whistle blew
and the quick climb
into daylight ended, there
was always on the faces

of the workers, and the faces
of the ponies, just
for an instant as the eyes adjusted,
a look of fear,

as if through the brains of the horses,
in the stunned realization
of predators, prey,
passed a sudden challenge:
So this is what must be survived—
and in the brains of the miners,
drawn back to that
green and wind-streaked beauty:
So this is what must be survived.

THE SKIN-BOATS: 1830

Back from the pin-tipped, eastern peninsula, back over
the basin of podzols and black earth, forests
and fodder crops, just outside the gates of St. Petersburg,
a thin hound skimmed through the grasses,
its bones almost hollow, weightless, its
flapping, weightless hair almost the grasses.
And circled a little cheering crowd, those few
in the foreground, sunburned and fattened, about to begin

their trip back. The long land took the color
of chestnuts. Ice buckled, broke, where the Sea of Okhotsk
curled under the Pacific. This year they would search
the Marquesas, snow squalls warming to vapor,
oilskins abandoned, sweaters and high-boots, the murmurs
of livestock floating up through the deck boards
as the sea turned slowly from slate to lime.

A glisten, then, on the lips and shoulders,
on the shadowy skin-boats lashed to the railing.
Brought on for the shallow waters, Aleut-boats: a shaving
of whalebone, a sheath of seal-hide, a wash
of clear fat, and thrummed by the trade winds,
the thin vessels trembled like reeds.

Like ghost hammocks, someone said, then pointed beyond
from his own plump sling, past his sleepy companions swaying
from the deck-works, past the border of rippling skin-boats

to the stars. *Wolf. Centaur. Hydra.* And slowly
the others began, tracing again the fabulous

shapes, visible or not. Scorpion, raven, then a hand-plow
perhaps, perhaps a glove or larch tree:
just over each face, the self with its jagged past
almost a constellation.

With the motion of whales the islands surfaced.
Sank and surfaced. Grew through one night to a green wall.
The skin-boats were lowered, legs slipped
through the glistening hatches, the glistening sheaths—

turned gradually useless. Whale fat, the flat, equatorial
sun, then sea licking over the pulpy seams. . . .
They stroked for a moment. Glided. Stroked, glided.
For a moment almost weightless, almost
wind or sea-tern—pale water, the crimson shore-scrub
brushing their shoulders—not otherworldly, but
other. Before the boats filled, the legs touched down.

STRIKE

First the salt was removed,
then the axes and powderhorns,
the blankets, jerky, shot-pouches, gourds,
the kettles and muslin, the burlap torsos of
cornmeal, and the wagons hauled on the coil of rope,
hand over hand, up
the last granite face of the High Sierra,
dangling, wobbling fat in that wind like lake bass,

then the oxen, pushed up the spidery trail—
in the concave crooks of their shanks,
the mules, centered and pushed—

and then it was all restored.

Soon the nut pines yielded to scrub pines, the wind
to the screams of the handcarts—
wooden axles, wooden wheel hubs,
day after day, the haunting, wooden voices.

Now and then, the lowland flashed up
through the trees, russet and gold-filled:
Ophir, Mineral Bar, the American River. Then
the scrub pines gave way to the black oaks, the wistful
manzanitas. On the bank of a river-fork
someone knelt, pinched the gravel,
plump and auriferous. Two others
talked of their journey, and the journey
of gold, of their last descent and that climbing:

fold-fault and lifting, erosion,
glaciation, explosion,
the magma and silica scratching upwards,

pin-step by pin-step to meet them.
All night the rain washed over the wagons,
cut down through the wheel ruts and fire-pits,
the powdery topsoil, as if to say
Deeper, just a little deeper,
and in the morning, pulled up in the muzzles
of mules, dangling in the grassy root-tips,
that gold dust, that ending.

OFF THE ALEUTIAN CHAIN

There is the sound of hail washed over a porthole, but
originating deeper, past the bunks
and galley, out
from the ship's icy center.
A door is opened. There—
it is the resonant swashing of claws:
king crabs in the hold stroking over one another,
their thousand bodies black and luminous.

This stroking, this echo of the weather,
is echoed again, just above, in a shuffle of limp cards.
Flushed and exhausted, the fishermen
slump from their chairs. Their hands

and the wide bracelets of skin above their wrists,
have weathered to the color of salmon gills.
At their elbows are bottles of rye,
white cheese; here and there, the dried carcasses
of tea bags, like huge, toppled moths.

One man is smiling. Slowly,

he snaps down a trio of flat queens.
Judith, he laughs. *Rachel. The steamy Argine.*
And it is then, summoned by name, by chance,
that these women brush through:
powdered, good-natured,
their ruffs and twills slightly acrid,

their faces a patchwork of circumstance, history,
unique in the mind of each fisherman.

They are gone in an instant, like the memory of
hail. Outside, the night sky is clearing.
Frigid winds and the winter sea-spray
have coated the ship with ice. Everything—
the spars and rigging, the mosaic
of dredges, trawl lines—is turning to ice.

No one is threatened. It is winter.

The ship simply cups its vertical cargo—
these swimmers and queens—their
parentheses of water—
rides with it into the morning.

About the Author

Linda Bierds, whose awards include a National Endowment for the Arts Fellowship in Poetry, an Artist Trust Foundation of Washington Fellowship in Poetry, and a Pushcart Prize in Poetry, has had her work published in such magazines and literary reviews as *The New Yorker, The Massachusetts Review, The Hudson Review, The New England Review and Bread Loaf Quarterly,* and *Poetry Northwest.* Her first volume of poetry, *Flights of the Harvest-Mare,* was among the hundred books in a special exhibit, New American Writing, sponsored by the National Endowment and exhibited at the 1986 Frankfurt Book Fair.

Ms. Bierds, who spent her early years in Anchorage, Alaska, lives in Seattle, Washington, where she edits the publications of the University of Washington's Women's Information Center. She has also taught poetry in the schools under the auspices of the Washington State Arts Commission and worked as a docent at Seattle's Woodland Park Zoo.